At the Construction Site

Look, a Backhoe!

By Julia Jaske

2 A backhoe can dig up.

A backhoe can dump out.

4   A backhoe can dig up dirt.

A backhoe can dump out dirt.

A backhoe can dig up soil.

A backhoe can dump out soil.

8 A backhoe can dig up sand.

A backhoe can dump out sand.

10 A backhoe can dig up the road.

A backhoe can dump out
the road.

12 A backhoe can dig up concrete.

A backhoe can dump out
concrete.

Word List

backhoe   dirt   road

dig   soil   concrete

dump   sand

A backhoe can dig up.

A backhoe can dump out.

A backhoe can dig up dirt.

A backhoe can dump out dirt.

A backhoe can dig up soil.

A backhoe can dump out soil.

A backhoe can dig up sand.

A backhoe can dump out sand.

A backhoe can dig up the road.

A backhoe can dump out the road.

A backhoe can dig up concrete.

A backhoe can dump out concrete.

CHERRY BLOSSOM PRESS

Published in the United States of America by Cherry Lake Publishing Group
Ann Arbor, Michigan
www.cherrylakepublishing.com

Photo Credits: © Attapon Thana/Shutterstock, cover, 1, 14; © Oleksandr Kostiuchenko/Shutterstock, back cover; © Dmitry Kalinovsky/Shutterstock, 2; © Deep Desert Photography/Shutterstock, 3; © Dmitry Kalinovsky/Shutterstock, 4; © TFoxFoto/Shutterstock, 5; © Rob Wilson/Shutterstock, 6; © Valentin Valkov/Shutterstock, 7; © TheHighestQualityImages/Shutterstock, 8; © Dmitry Kalinovsky/Shutterstock, 9; © Ivto/Shutterstock, 10; © leedsn/Shutterstock, 11; © Semyon Nazarov/Shutterstock, 12; © taylanozgurefe/Shutterstock, 13

Cherry Blossom Press is an imprint of Cherry Lake Publishing Group.

Library of Congress Cataloging-in-Publication Data

Names: Jaske, Julia, author.
Title: Look, a backhoe! / by Julia Jaske.
Description: Ann Arbor, Michigan : Cherry Lake Publishing, [2021] | Series:
   At the Construction Site
Identifiers: LCCN 2021007812 (print) | LCCN 2021007813 (ebook) | ISBN
   9781534188228 (Paperback) | ISBN 9781534189621 (PDF) | ISBN
   9781534191020 (eBook)
Subjects: LCSH: Backhoes–Juvenile literature. | Illustrated children's
   books.
Classification: LCC TA735 .J37 2021 (print) | LCC TA735 (ebook) | DDC
   621.8/65–dc23
LC record available at https://lccn.loc.gov/2021007812
LC ebook record available at https://lccn.loc.gov/2021007813

Printed in the United States of America
Corporate Graphics